GREEN WORKBOOK PART #1

TABLE OF CONTENTS

FROM THE AUTHOR	PG 3
GREEN WORKBOOK PART #2 TABLE OF CONTENTS	PG 4
GREETINGS AND FAREWELLS	PG 5
GREETINGS AND FAREWELLS	PG 6
GREETINGS AND FAREWELLS	PG 7
GREETINGS AND FAREWELLS	PG 8
GREETINGS AND FAREWELLS	PG 9
CLASSROOM COMMANDS	PG 10
CLASSROOM COMMANDS	PG 11
CLASSROOM COMMANDS	PG 12
CLASSROOM COMMANDS	PG 13
CLASSROOM VOCABULARY	PG 14
CLASSROOM VOCABULARY	PG 15
CLASSROOM VOCABULARY	PG 16
CLASSROOM VOCABULARY	PG 17
NUMBERS 1 – 10	PG 18
NUMBERS 1 – 10	PG 19
NUMBERS 1 – 10	PG 20
NUMBERS 1 – 10	PG 21
NUMBERS 1 – 10	PG 22
VOWELS	PG 23
ALPHABET	PG 24
ALPHABET	PG 25
ALPHABET	PG 26
ALPHABET	PG 27
COLORS	PG 28
COLORS	PG 29
COLORS	PG 30
SUBJECT PRONOUNS	PG 31
PLACES AROUND THE SCHOOL	PG 32
PLACES AROUND THE SCHOOL	PG 33
SCHOOL SUBJECTS	PG 34
SCHOOL SUBJECTS	PG 35

Published by World Language Institute, Inc. Copyright protected   SPANISH   GREEN WORKBOOK # 1

NUMBERS 11-15	PG 36
NUMBERS 16 – 20	PG 37
NUMBERS 11 – 20	PG 38
NUMBERS 11 – 20	PG 39
MONTHS	PG 40
MONTHS	PG 41
MONTHS	PG 42
DAYS	PG 43
DAYS	PG 44
PARTS OF THE BODY	PG 45
PARTS OF THE FACE	PG 46
PARTS OF THE BODY AND FACE	PG 47
PARTS OF THE BODY AND FACE	PG 48
DESCRIPTIONS	PG 49
DESCRIPTIONS	PG 50
FAMILY	PG 51
FAMILY	PG 52
FAMILY	PG 53
NUMBERS 20 - 30	PG 54
NUMBERS 20 - 30	PG 55
NUMBERS 20 - 30	PG 56
CLOTHES	PG 57
CLOTHES	PG 58
CLOTHES	PG 59
WEATHER AND SEASONS	PG 60
WEATHER AND SEASONS	PG 61
WEATHER AND SEASONS	PG 62
CULTURE: HOLIDAYS	PG 63
CULTURE: HOLIDAYS	PG 64

Nombre_____   Fecha_____

"From the Author"

Biography:
Celia Sandoval is a certified Spanish teacher and holds a master's degree in education. She has been teaching for over twelve years Pk-12. Celia's children are fully bilingual and credit can be attributed to their early immersion in the languages. Her passion for languages and her love for this country have motivated her to promote the learning of languages during the last ten years of her life.

From the author:
I want to congratulate you because you are taking the first step of a long journey. Learning a second language takes time, practice, repetition, and dedication. It's just like learning to play a new instrument. You will not see the improvement over night but your child is learning, trust me. As a witness to the challenges and disappointments that students and parents have to overcome to learn a second language, I know becoming bilingual is achievable with dedication and perseverance.

Learning a second language opens a window of opportunities, but it is not just the learning of the language itself, it is also the understanding and appreciation of other cultures, foods, traditions, religions, and politics. Worldwide, people of all races and cultures are educating themselves in English, as well as the American culture. The world is progressing as its people master the art of languages and the beauty of cultures. How can we be expected to oversee a world when we have not studied its vast sea of cultures and languages?

I believe that early language exposure is the foundation to speaking a second language fluently. The younger the children start their journey of learning a second language the better and easier will be for them.

Sincerely,

Celia Sandoval

I would like to recognize and thank Krystal Scoggins for providing her artistic talent and dedication to World Language Institute.

Nombre_____   Fecha_____

"GREEN WORKBOOK PART #2 Table of Contents"

FURNITURE
NUMBERS 40-100
TELLING TIME
PROFESSIONS
HARDWARE TOOLS
PLACES IN THE CITY
RECREATIONAL PLACES
TRANSPORTATION
SPORTS
ACTION WORDS
PETS
FARM
ZOO
VEGETABLES
FRUITS
KITCHEN UTENSILS
BEVERAGES
ORDERING IN A RESTAURANT
CULTURE: FOOD

Nombre_____   Fecha_____

"Greetings and Farewells" Study Guide
Directions: Use this guide to study your vocabulary words.

Hola

Adiós

¿Cómo estás?

Bien

Nombre_____   Fecha_____

"Greetings and Farewells" Study Guide

Mal

Así- así

¿Cómo te llamas?

Me llamo…

Nombre_____   Fecha_____

"Greetings and Farewells" Handwriting Practice Sheets

Directions: Use a pencil to trace each word below using your best handwriting. Write each word three times on the line provided.

1) ¿Cómo te llamas? *(what is your name?)*

2) así, así? *(so-so)*

3) adiós *(good bye)*

4) Hola *(Hello)*

Published by World Language Institute, Inc. Copyright protected   SPANISH   GREEN WORKBOOK #1   Page 7

Nombre_____   Fecha_____

"Greetings and Farewells" Handwriting Practice Sheets

5) bien *(good)*

6) Me llamo *(My name is)*

7) mal *(bad)*

8) ¿Cómo estás? *(How are you?)*

Nombre_____   Fecha_____

"Greetings and Farewells" Matching

Directions: Draw a line of the word that best matches the meaning.

 My name is	¿Cómo estás?
 How are you?	¿Cómo te llamas?
 good	adiós
 good bye	así, así
 Hello	bien
 bad	Hola
 so-so	mal
 What is your name?	Me llamo

Nombre_____   Fecha_____

"Classroom commands" Study Guide
Directions: Use this guide to study your vocabulary words.

Abre la puerta: Open the door

Cierra la puerta: Close the door

Escucha: Listen

Levanta la mano: Raise your hand

Nombre_____   Fecha_____

"Classroom commands" Study Guide

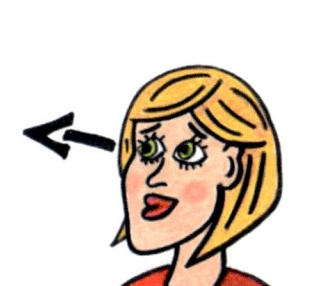

Mira: Look

Escribe: Write

Siéntate: Sit-down

Silencio: Silence

Nombre_____   Fecha_____

"Classroom Commands" Handwriting Practice Sheets

Directions: Use a pencil to trace each word below using your best handwriting. Write each word three times on the line provided.

1) Escribe *(Write)*

---

2) Mira *(Look)*

---

3) Abre la puerta *(Open the door)*

---

4) Cierra la puerta *(Close the door)*

Published by World Language Institute, Inc. Copyright protected   SPANISH   GREEN WORKBOOK #1 Page 12

Nombre_____   Fecha_____

"Classroom Commands" Handwriting Practice Sheets

5) Escucha   *(Listen)*

6) Levanta la mano   *(Raise your hand)*

7) Silencio   *(Silence)*

10) Siéntate   *(Si- down)*

Nombre_____   Fecha_____

"Classroom Vocabulary" Study Guide
Directions: Use this guide to study your vocabulary words.

el cuaderno: notebook

la mesa: table

el lápiz: pencil

el libro: book

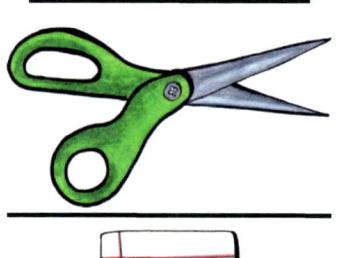

las tijeras: sicssors

el papel: paper

Nombre_____   Fecha_____

"Classroom Vocabulary" Study Guide

el pegamento: glue

la pluma: pen

la computadora: computer

la silla: chair

Published by World Language Institute, Inc. Copyright protected   SPANISH   GREEN WORKBOOK #1 Page 15

Nombre_____ Fecha_____

"Classroom Vocabulary" Matching
Directions: Draw a line from the word to the correct picture.

el libro

el cuaderno

las tijeras

la mesa

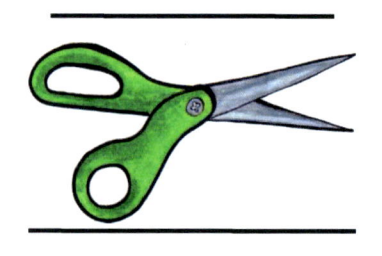

el lápiz

Nombre_____   Fecha_____

"Classroom Vocabulary" Matching

la silla

la pluma

el papel

el pegamento

la computadora

Nombre_____   Fecha_____

"Numbers 1-10" Study Guide
Directions: Use this guide to study your vocabulary words.

1 uno

2 dos

3 tres

4 cuatro

5 cinco

Nombre_____ Fecha_____

"Numbers 1-10" Study Guide

seis

siete

ocho

nueve

diez

Nombre_____ Fecha_____

"Numbers 1-10" Pronunciation
Directions: Count the animals out loud

1 uno	2 dos
3 tres	4 cuatro
5 cinco	6 seis

Nombre_____   Fecha_____

"Numbers 1-10" Pronunciation
Directions: Count the animals out loud

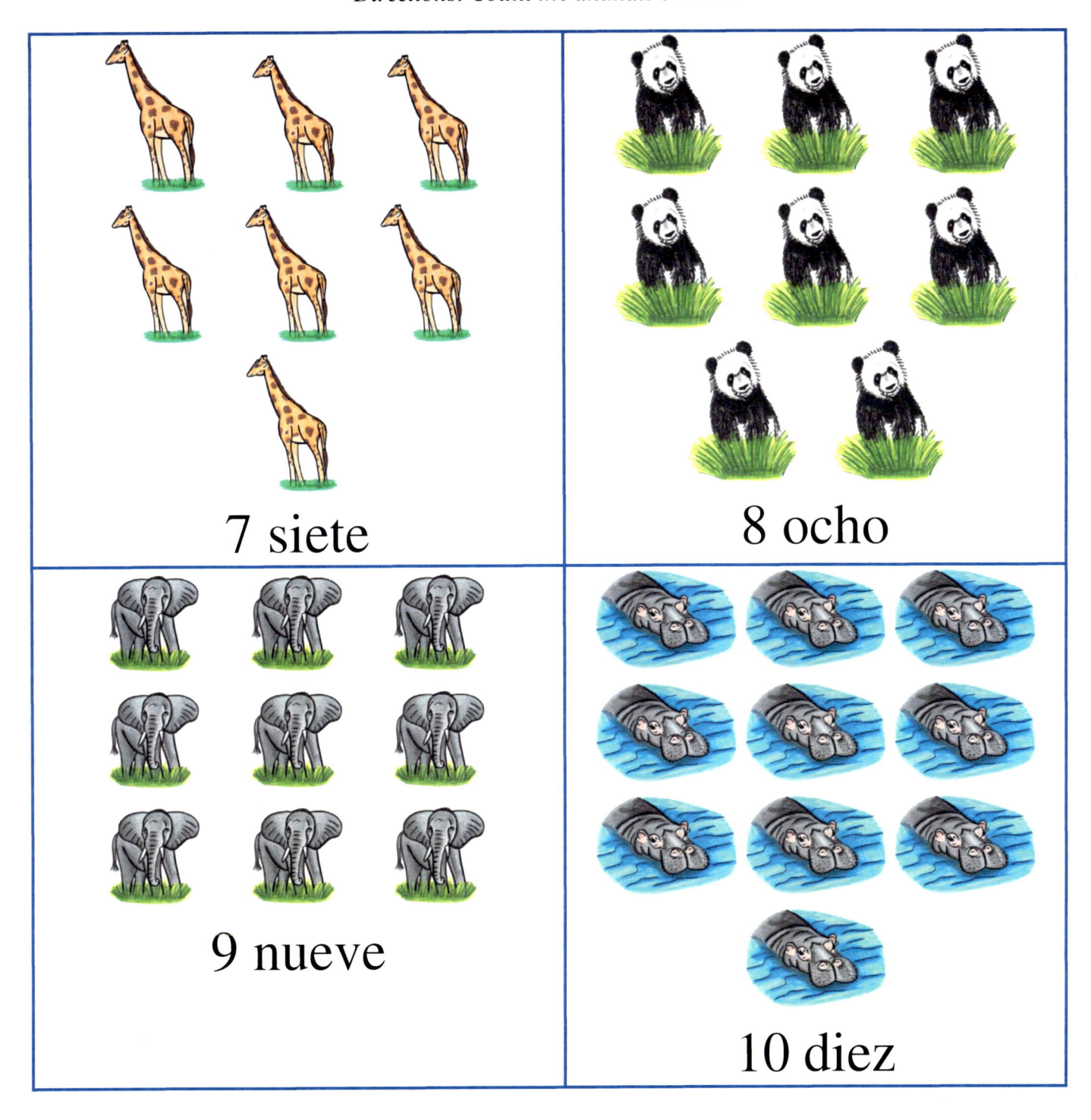

7 siete

8 ocho

9 nueve

10 diez

Nombre_____   Fecha_____

"Numbers 1-10" Draw
Directions: Draw the correct number of circles in each box

uno			seis	
dos			siete	
tres			ocho	
cuatro			nueve	
cinco			diez	

Nombre_____   Fecha_____

"Vowels" Study Guide

Directions: Use this guide to study your vocabulary words.

A   Aa   **La Abeja**

E   Ee   **El establo**

I   Ii   **El invierno**

O   Oo   **La oveja**

U   Uu   **Las uvas**

CANCION DE LAS VOCALES

Ahí viene la **A**, le gusta bailar con sus dos patitas, muy abiertas, sin parar.

Le sigue la **E**, moviendo los pies, el palo del medio es más corto, como ves.

Ahí viene la **I**, también la **O**. Una delgadita y la otra gorda porque ya comió.

Y para acabar, llegó la **U**, como la cuerda en la que siempre saltas tú.

Nombre_____ Fecha_____

"The Alphabet" Color and Circle

Directions: Color the letters. Then circle the matching letter in each row.

A a	La abeja		A L A C D a e d A L
B b	El búho		B d z b a c D L W B
C c	La calabaza		C d B D e c a C b c
CH ch	El champiñón		Ch d e ch f ll w ch
D d	El dibujo		E B Ch D ll d D d
E e	El establo		G e Z E F I O p E B e
F f	La flor		A E f f Q f G O f f R

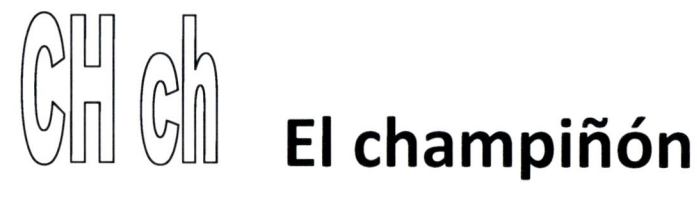

Published by World Language Institute, Inc. Copyright protected   SPANISH   GREEN WORKBOOK #1 Page 24

Nombre_____ Fecha_____

"The Alphabet" Color and Circle

G g La guitarra — F G g O A a F g G O

H h La hamburguesa — U H o h F h G H I

I i El invierno — J H I i p j i R A a I

J j El jardín — G I J i j I L M A O o J

K k El koala — O K I j k L ll M k K

L l El lápiz — K J j H L i L l J A a

Ll ll La lluvia — L L M ll N J j j p L ll

M m La mariposa — N n M O W w m N

Published by World Language Institute, Inc. Copyright protected   SPANISH   GREEN WORKBOOK #1 Page 25

Nombre_____   Fecha_____

"The Alphabet" Color and Circle

N n El nopal — M n O W N M n N A

Ñ ñ El niño — P N m **ñ w ñ M ñ**

O o La oveja — O J j P Q q o U u O

P p El pollo — O p Q R r s T q N b

Q q El queso — B b Q p Q q P N q

R r El reloj — S T s U R T r R T P

Rr rr El perro — O p Q R r s T q N b

S s El sol — A s T S R t U X B s

Published by World Language Institute, Inc. Copyright protected   SPANISH   GREEN WORKBOOK #1 Page 26

Nombre_____ Fecha_____

"The Alphabet" Color and Circle

T t La tortuga — J T S t X t R V v

U u Las uvas — V X u v U A a u

V v La vaca — U V u x v T U v

X x El xilófono — X R O P p U x V x

Y y El yoyo — X y x Y K R z P Q

Z z El zapato — F Z f z N s Z S n

Nombre_____   Fecha_____

"Colors" Study Guide

Directions: Use this guide to study your vocabulary words.

rosado	pink
rojo	red
anaranjado	orange
verde	green
amarillo	yellow
morado	purple
azul	blue

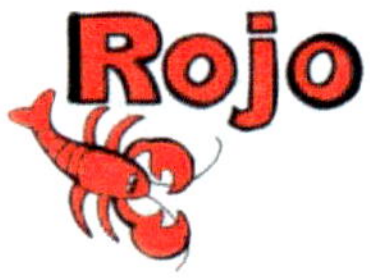

Published by World Language Institute, Inc. Copyright protected   SPANISH   GREEN WORKBOOK #1

Nombre_____   Fecha_____

"Colors" Coloring

Directions: Say the words out loud. Color the word with the correct color.

Rosado

Rojo

Anaranjado

Verde

Amarillo

Morado

Azul

Nombre_____   Fecha_____

"Colors" Handwriting Practice Sheets

Directions: Use a pencil to trace each word below using your best handwriting. Write each word three times on the line provided.

1) azul   *(blue)*

   azul _____

2) amarillo   *(yellow)*

   amarillo _____

3) blanco   *(white)*

   blanco _____

4) verde   *(green)*

   verde _____

5) rosado   *(pink)*

   rosado _____

6) morado   *(purple)*

   morado _____

7) rojo   *(red)*

   rojo _____

8) anaranjado   *(orange)*

   anaranjado _____

Published by World Language Institute, Inc. Copyright protected   SPANISH   GREEN WORKBOOK #1

Nombre_____   Fecha_____

"Subject Pronouns" Study Guide
Directions: Use this guide to study your vocabulary words.

Yo: I	
Tú: You (informal) Your sister, brother, friend, a young person	
Él: He	
Ella: She	
Usted: You (formal) Your principal, teacher, an older person	

Nombre_____ Fecha_____

"Places Around the School" Study Guide
Directions: Use this guide to study your vocabulary words.

La escuela	school	
El estadio	stadium	
La oficina	office	
La clínica	clinic	
La cafetería	cafeteria	
El baño	bathroom	

Nombre_____   Fecha_____

"Places Around the School" Our school

Directions: Draw a picture of a school showing the school place named at the bottom of the page. Label the places in Spanish.

La escuela	La oficina	El baño
El estadio	La cafetería	La clínica

Nombre_____   Fecha_____

"School Subjects" Study Guide
Directions: Use this guide to study your vocabulary words.

las ciencias		science
la música		music
las matemáticas		math
el arte		art
el español		Spanish
el inglés		English

Nombre_____ Fecha_____

"School Subjects" Word Shapes

Directions: At the bottom of the page is a list of words. Print the words in the empty boxes above. The shape of the word must match the shape of the boxes.

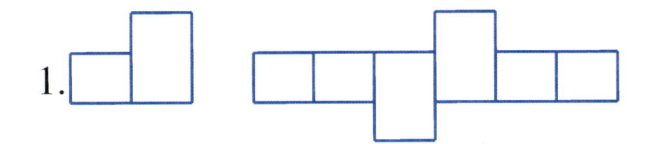

1.

2.

3.

4.

5.

6.

1. English
2. Spanish
3. music
4. math
5. science
6. art

el español	la música	las ciencias	el inglés
el arte	las matemáticas		

Nombre_____   Fecha_____

"Numbers: 11-15" Study Guide
Directions: Use this guide to study your vocabulary words.

once: eleven

doce: twelve

trece: thirteen

catorce: fourteen

quince: fifteen

Nombre_____   Fecha_____

"Numbers: 16-20" Study Guide
Directions: Use this guide to study your vocabulary words.

dieciséis:
sixteen

diecisiete:
seventeen

dieciocho:
eighteen

diecinueve:
nineteen

veinte:
twenty

Nombre_____   Fecha_____

"Numbers: 11-20" Circle

Directions: Say each word out lout. Circle the number that tells the meaning of the word.

veinte	20	11	12
once	18	15	19
diecinueve	16	19	18
doce	12	15	16
quince	14	12	15
dieciséis	16	20	19
trece	11	12	13
diecisiete	18	19	17
dieciocho	19	20	18
catorce	11	14	13

Nombre_____   Fecha_____

"Numbers 11-20" Vocabulary Color-In

Directions: Find the definition that matches each number in the picture, then find the word that matches that definition. Finally, use crayons, markers, or colored pencils to color in the numbered space with the color listed beside the word.

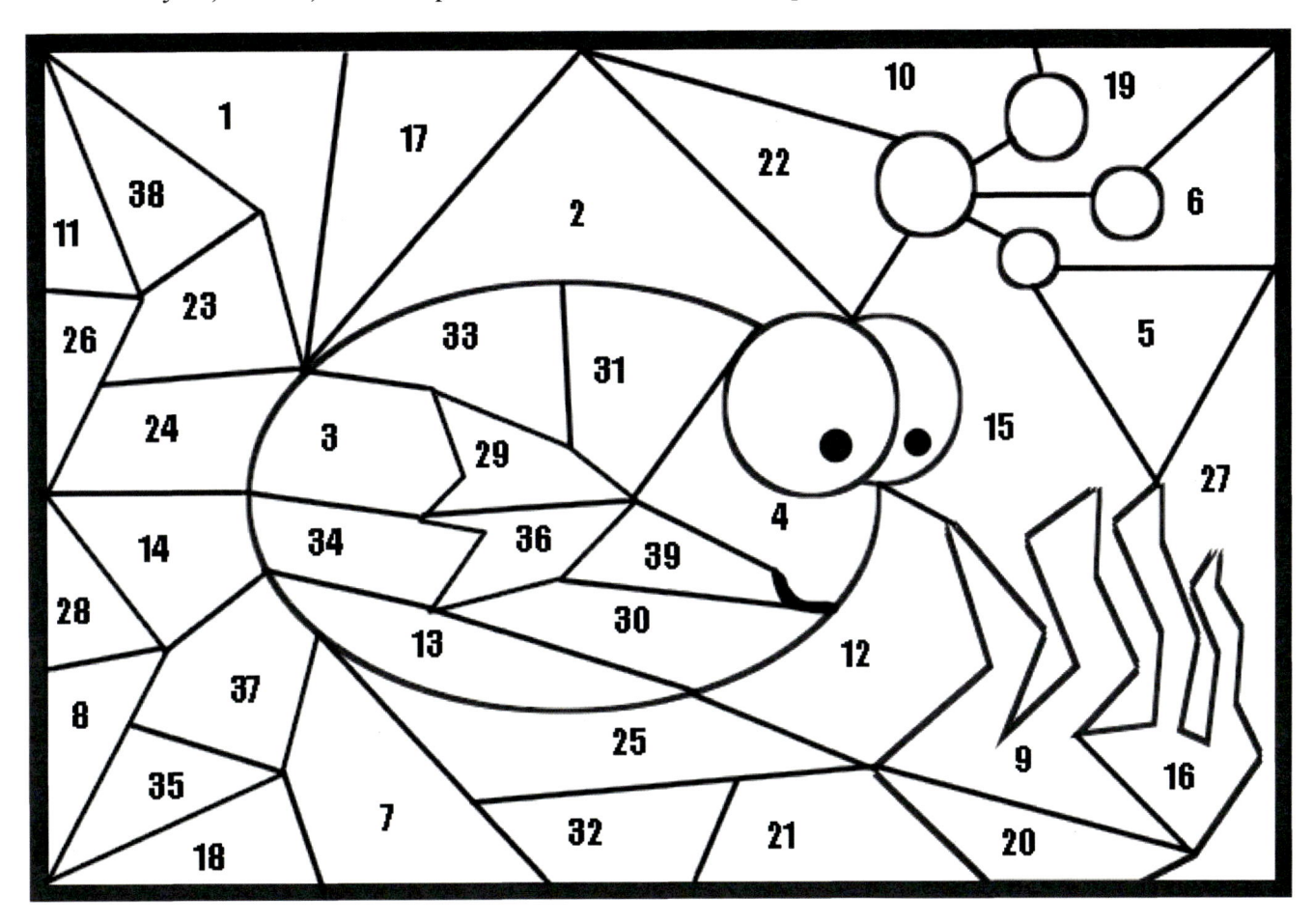

Word Bank:

(AMARILLO)-quince   (VERDE)-trece   (AZUL)-once   (AMARILLO)-diecinueve
(AMARILLO)-quince   (VERDE)-dieciséis   (AZUL)-catorce   (AZUL)-veinte
(AMARILLO)-quince   (AMARILLO)-diecinueve

Published by World Language Institute, Inc. Copyright protected   SPANISH   GREEN WORKBOOK #1 Page 39

Nombre_____   Fecha_____

"Months" Study Guide

Directions: Use this guide to study your vocabulary words.

enero	enero	January
febrero	febrero	February
marzo	marzo	March
abril	abril	April
mayo	mayo	May
junio	junio	June
julio	julio	July
agosto	agosto	August
septiembre	septiembre	September
octubre	octubre	October
noviembre	noviembre	November
diciembre	diciembre	December

Nombre_____   Fecha_____

"Months" Handwriting Practice Sheets

Directions: Use a pencil to trace each word below using your best handwriting. Write each word three times on the line provided.

enero *(January)*

febrero *(February)*

marzo *(March)*

abril *(April)*

mayo *(May)*

junio *(June)*

Nombre_____   Fecha_____

"Months" Handwriting Practice Sheets

julio   *(July)*

agosto   *(August)*

septiembre   *(September)*

octubre   *(October)*

noviembre   *(November)*

diciembre   *(December)*

Nombre_____ Fecha_____

"Days" Study Guide

Directions: Use this guide to study your vocabulary words.

lunes:		**Monday**
martes:		**Tuesday**
miércoles:		**Wednesday**
jueves:		**Thursday**
viernes:		**Friday**
sábado:		**Saturday**
domingo:		**Sunday**

Nombre_____   Fecha_____

"Days" Word Shapes

Directions: At the bottom of the page is a list of words. Print the words in the empty boxes above. The shape of the word must match the shape of the boxes.

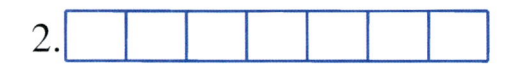

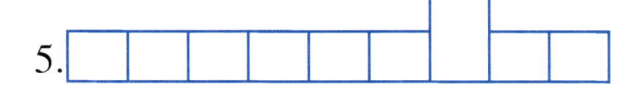

1.
2.
3.
4.
5.
6.
7.

1. Sunday
2. Friday
3. Tuesday
4. Saturday
5. Wednesday
6. Monday
7. Thursday

| miércoles | jueves | viernes | sábado |
| domingo | lunes | martes | |

Nombre_____   Fecha_____

"Parts of the Body" Study Guide
Directions: Use this guide to study your vocabulary words.

el brazo	arm
la pierna	leg
el pie	foot
la mano	hand
los dedos	fingers
los dedos de los pies	toes

Nombre_____   Fecha_____

"Parts of the Face" Study Guide

Directions: Use this guide to study your vocabulary words.

la cabeza		head
el pelo		hair
La nariz		nose
la boca		mouth
los ojos		Eyes
la oreja		ear

Nombre_____ Fecha_____

"Parts of the Body and Face" My body

Directions: Draw a picture of yourself. Label the places in Spanish.

el brazo	los dedos	la nariz
la pierna	los dedos de los pies	la boca
el pie	la cabeza	los ojos
la mano	el pelo	la oreja

Nombre_____   Fecha_____

"Parts of the Body and Face" Crossword

Directions: Using the Across and Down clues, write the correct words in the numbered grid below.

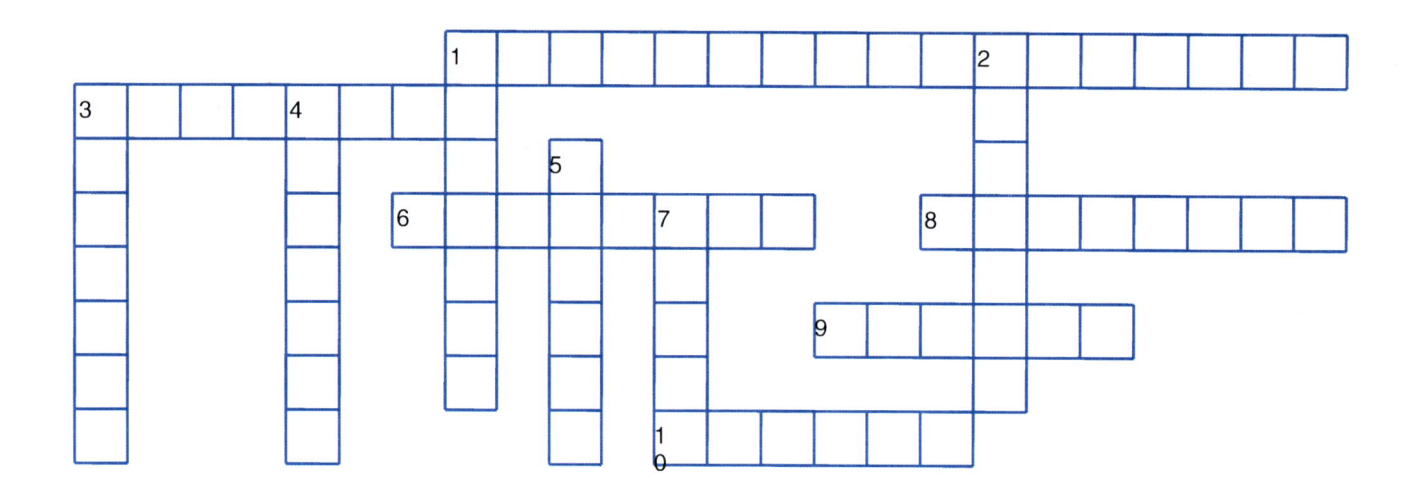

ACROSS	DOWN
1. toes	1. nose
3. leg	2. eyes
6. head	3. ear
8. fingers	4. arm
9. mouth	5. hand
10. hair	7. foot

los ojos	la oreja	la mano	la nariz
los dedos de los pies	la pierna	los dedos	el pie
la cabeza	el pelo	el brazo	la boca

Nombre_____   Fecha_____

"Descriptions" Study Guide

Directions: Directions: Use this guide to study your vocabulary words.

bonito/a	pretty
alto/a	tall
feo/a	ugly
delgado/a	skinny
gordo/a	fat
viejo/a	old
bajo/a	short

Nombre_____   Fecha_____

"Descriptions" Crossword

Directions: Using the Across and Down clues, write the correct words in the numbered grid below.

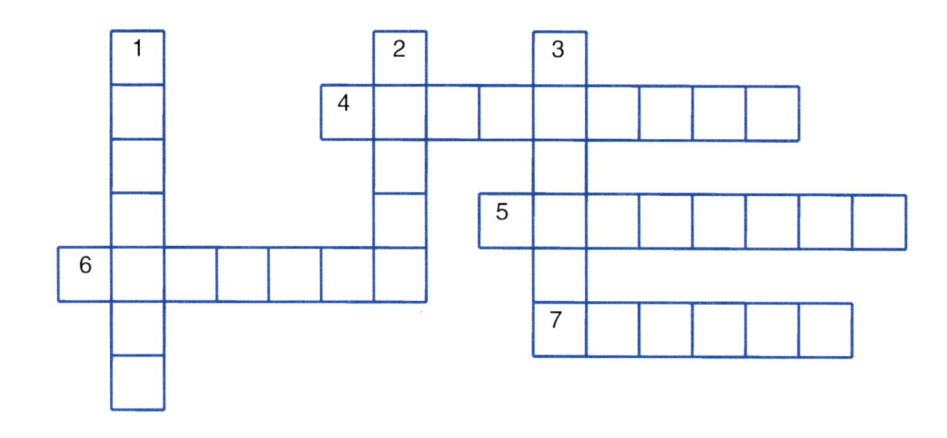

ACROSS
4. skinny
5. pretty
6. fat
7. tall

DOWN
1. old
2. ugly
3. short

| feo/a | alto/a | viejo/a | bonito/a |
| bajo/a | delgado/a | gordo/a | |

Nombre_____   Fecha_____

"Family" Study Guide

Directions: Use this guide to study your vocabulary words.

el abuelo: grandfather		**la familia**: family	
el hermano: brother		**el padre**: father	
la abuela: grandmother		**los abuelos**: grandparents	
la hermana: sister		**la madre**: mother	

Published by World Language Institute, Inc. Copyright protected   SPANISH   GREEN WORKBOOK #1 Page 51

Nombre_____   Fecha_____

"Family" Word Meaning

Directions: Say each word out loud. Circle the picture that shows the meaning of each word.

el abuelo:

el hermano:

la abuela:

la hermana:

Nombre_____   Fecha_____

"Family" Word Meaning

Directions: Say each word out loud. Circle the picture that shows the meaning of each word.

la familia:

el padre:

los abuelos:

la madre:

Nombre_____   Fecha_____

"Numbers: 20-30" Study Guide

Directions: Use this guide to study your vocabulary words.

		veinte		twenty
	veintiuno	twenty-one		veintiséis	twenty-six
	veintidós	twenty-two		veintisiete	twenty-seven
	veintitrés	twenty-three		veintiocho	twenty-eight
	veinticuatro	twenty-four		veintinueve	twenty-nine
	veinticinco	twenty-five		treinta	thirty

Published by World Language Institute, Inc. Copyright protected   SPANISH   GREEN WORKBOOK #1 Page 54

Nombre_____   Fecha_____

"Numbers: 20-30" Matching Activity

Directions: Clues are listed below. Print the word that matches the clue on the blank line by the clue.

1. _____ twenty-four
2. _____ twenty-nine
3. _____ twenty-three
4. _____ twenty-six
5. _____ twenty-two

6. _____ twenty-eight
7. _____ twenty
8. _____ twenty-seven
9. _____ thirty
10. _____ twenty-five

veintisiete	veintiséis	veinte	veintinueve
veintitrés	veintidós	veintiocho	veinticuatro
treinta	veinticinco		

Nombre_____   Fecha_____

"Numbers: 20-30" Counting On
Directions: Rewrite the number words in the Word Bank in order

veintisiete	veintiséis	veinte	veintinueve
veintitrés	veintidós	veintiocho	veinticuatro
treinta	veinticinco		

21 _____
22 _____
23 _____
24 _____
25 _____
26 _____
27 _____
28 _____
29 _____
30 _____

Nombre_____   Fecha_____

"Clothes" Study Guide
Directions: Use this guide to study your vocabulary words.

el gorro: cap	**la falda**: skirt
el vestido: dress	**las botas**: boots
la blusa: blouse	**los jeans**: jeans
los zapatos: shoes	**los pantalones**: slacks
la camisa: shirt	**los pijamas**: pajamas

Nombre_____   Fecha_____

"Clothes" Drawings
Directions: Draw a picture that matches the word.

el gorro:	**la falda**:
el vestido:	**las botas**:
la blusa:	**los jeans**:
los zapatos:	**los pantalones**:
la camisa:	**los pijamas**:

Nombre_____   Fecha_____

"Clothes" Word Search

Directions: At the bottom of the page is a list of words. These words are hidden in the puzzle. The words have been placed horizontally, vertically, or diagonally - frontwards or backwards. When you locate a word, draw a circle around it.

B	E	L	G	O	R	R	O	F	L	V	N	Y
L	A	B	L	U	S	A	L	Z	A	T	G	N
X	L	A	F	A	L	D	A	X	S	N	C	L
K	Z	T	B	R	Y	O	T	K	B	M	C	O
L	O	S	P	A	N	T	A	L	O	N	E	S
L	A	C	A	M	I	S	A	T	T	V	I	J
P	L	O	S	P	I	J	A	M	A	S	M	E
K	Q	W	J	O	R	K	H	S	S	V	G	A
Y	M	E	L	V	E	S	T	I	D	O	V	N
Q	T	L	O	S	Z	A	P	A	T	O	S	S
F	E	M	D	T	S	H	M	P	W	J	B	V

1. dress
2. skirt
3. pajamas
4. shoes
5. boots
6. blouse
7. cap
8. slacks
9. shirt
10. jeans

los pijamas	los jeans	los pantalones
el gorro	la camisa	las botas
el vestido	la blusa	la falda
los zapatos		

Nombre_____   Fecha_____

"Weather and Seasons" Study Guide
Directions: Use this guide to study your vocabulary words.

Weather/el tiempo	Seasons/las estaciones del año
hace calor: it's hot	**el invierno**: winter
hace frío: it's cold	**el otoño**: fall
hace sol: it's sunny	**el verano**: summer
nieva: it snows	**la primavera**: spring

Nombre_____   Fecha_____

"Weather and Seasons" Handwriting Practice Sheets

Directions: Use a pencil to trace each word below using your best handwriting. Write each word three times on the line provided.

la primavera   *(spring)*

el verano   *(summer)*

hace frío   *(it is cold)*

el invierno   *(winter)*

el otoño   *(fall)*

nieva   *(snows)*

hace sol   *(it's sunny)*

hace calor   *(it's hot)*

Nombre_____ Fecha_____

"Weather and Seasons" Crossword

Directions: Using the Across and Down clues, write the correct words in the numbered grid below.

ACROSS
1. it's cold
2. winter
4. fall
5. it's hot
6. summer
7. spring

DOWN
1. it's sunny
3. it snows

| la primavera | nieva | hace frío | el invierno |
| hace sol | el verano | el otoño | hace calor |

Nombre_____   Fecha_____

"Holidays" Study Guide

Directions: Use this guide to study Spanish-speaking countries' holidays.

Jan 1
Año Nuevo, New Year's Day.

Jan 6
Día de los Reyes Magos or *Día de los Santos Reyes*. Traditionally the children receive gifts on this day rather than on Christmas.

May 5
Cinco de Mayo (México) commemorates the victory of Mexican forces over the French army at the Battle of Puebla

May 10
Día de las Madres, or Day of the Mothers, observed on this date in Mexico and other Latin-American countries.

Nov 1 & 2
Día de los Muertos or Day of the Dead (Mexico, Central America).

Dec 16-24
Las Posadas (Mexico, Guatemala and other Central American countries). Family and friends visit one another in their homes and enjoy conversations and traditional foods, and visitors sing carols.

Dec 24 & 25
La Nochebuena y la *Navidad*, Christmas Eve and Christmas.

Nombre_____ Fecha_____

"Holidays" Matching Activity

Directions: Clues are listed below. Print the word that matches the clue on the blank line by the clue.

1. _____ Cinco de mayo

2. _____ La Nochebuena y la Navidad

3. _____ Día de los muertos

4. _____ Día de las madres

5. _____ Día de los Reyes Mago

6. _____ Año Nuevo

7. _____ Las Posadas

May 5	November 1 & 2
December 16 - 24	May 10
December 24 & 25	January 1
January 6	